"The Don"
"Secret Agent Don"
Artist: Vanessa Wells
Insta: nesiw_
Email: nesiw@outlook.com

Contents

1: Youth
(Gioventù)
2: Cunning Lingus
(Cunni Lingia)
3: Compromise
(Compromesso)
4: Passion or Nothing
(Passione o Niente)
5: The Siren
(la Sirena)
6: Mas Turbation
(Mas Turbarsi)
7: Reprocipity
(Riprocipità)
8: V
9: I'm Arrogant
(Io Sono arrogante)
10: Domesticated
(Addomesticata)
11: Compromise verses Benefits
(Vantaggi versetti Compromesso)
12: Man....in Chaos
(Uomo ... nel Caos)
13: I Was Not a Good Friend
(Non ero un Buon Amico)
14: How Young Are You?
(Quanto Giovane se tu?)
15: Faceless
(Senza Faccia)
16: Women Have the Power
(Le Donne hanno il Potere)
17: You Can't Go Back
(Non Puoi Tornare Indietro)

Contents

18: The Creative Process
(Il Processo Creativo)
19: Are You Happy?
(Sei Felice?)
20: Sex is NOT LO♥E
(Il Sesso NON è Amore)
21: Relationships
(Relazioni)
22: Good Things Come to those that Wait
(Le Cose Buone Arrivano a Coloro che Aspettano)
23: Creative Disorder
(Disordine Creativo)
24: Make Me Happy
(Rendermi Felice)
25: Don't Sweat the Small Stuff
(Non Sudare le Piccole Cose)
26: I Don't Believe in Anything
(Io Non Credo a Niente)
27: Ska8er Girl
(Ragazza Ska8er)
28: Feelin' Groovy
(Sensazione di Groovy)
29: Mas Turbation
(Mas Turbarsi)
30: Lo♥e is a Commodity
(L'amore è una Merce)
31: I Live in My Head
(Vivo Nella Mia Testa)
32: Do Not Think
(Non Pensare)
33: Miriam is Dead
(Miriam è Morta)
34: I am the Tit Man
(Io sono il Tit Uomo)

Contents

35: I am a WOG: WOG Boy
36: Clothing Maketh the Man
(Vestiti Fa L'uomo)
37: Scars
(Cicatrici)
38: Rejection revisited
(Rigetto rivisitato)
39: A Poem for Bob
(Una Poesia per Bob)
40: The Only Thing We've Got Left is Sophistication
(L'unica cosa che ci Resta è la Sofisticazione)
41: Life is a Bummer, Sometimes
(La Vita è una Peccata, a Volte)
42: The Running Woman
(La Donna che Corre)
43: I Am Responsible
(Io Sono Responsabile)
44: Be Yourself
(Essere te Stesso)
45: Abused
(Abusata)
46: Toxic Positivity
(Positività Tossica)
47: Superstition
(Superstizione)
48: Are You Happy #2?
(Sei Felice #2?)
49: Wild Girls
(Ragazze Selvagge)
50: Bad Boy
(Cattivo Ragazzo)

Youth

(Gioventù)

My youth.
It was another lifetime ago.
Where has it gone?
Did it even really happen?
Or was it just a transient dream?
My *Youth*.

Lost opportunities.
Lost friends.
Lost Lo♥ers.
Lost Ideals.
Lost Principles.
Lost dreams.
Lost *Youth*.

The endless nights.
The endless conversations.
About Life, society & the meaning of *"Existence"*.
The smoke-filled garage of ...
...*dope,*
...*music,*
...*wine,*
...*song,*
...*girls (which were all in my head).*
...*idealism.*
My *"Idealistic" Youth*.

I squandered my *youth*.
I'm trying to make up for it now...
...but it's too late.
But unfortunately, it happens to all of us.
We have no choice in the matter.
This is the *"nature"* of *Youth*.
It cannot be captured.
Youth will ALWAYS be lost.
Youth is just a *"state of mind"*.

Oh, *Youth*!

*"I wish, I wish, I wish in vain.
That we could sit simply in that room again.
Ten thousand dollars at the drop of a hat.
I'd give it all gladly if our lives could be like that."*

"Bob Dylan's Dream" by Bob Dylan

Vito Radice ("The Don"), when he was 20 years old.
A curly, red-headed Southern Italian with freckles & fair skin

"The Don"
25.04.2021

Cunning Lingus

(Cunni Lingia)

Cunning Lingus.
Cunning tongue.
Cunning ficus.
Cunning fig.
Cunning Stunt.
Long tongue.
Playful tongue.
Skilful tongue.
Pleasuring tongue.

What a cunning stunt you are.
Can I carry out some *Cunning Lingus* on you?
It won't take long.
I'm very fast!
I like to use my tongue.
It can go into very interesting places!
Let it do what it does BEST!
Cunning Lingus!

It provides PLEASURE!
It knows exactly what to do.
It knows exactly where the pleasure spot is.
It knows exactly the right amount of pressure to apply.
It is the *"Cunning Lingus"* expert.

"I have a tongue & I can use it".
It's the longest tongue in the west.
It can get into all the nocks & crevices.
It has a very light *(when it is needed)*.
Give it a try.
I'm sure you'll be satisfied.
You'll be wanting more.
"Have tongue, will pleasure!"
My tongue's name is....
...."Cunning Lingus".

Inspired by Nick (from the now defunct "Glebe Tuckerbox")

"The Don"
25.04.2021

Compromise

(Compromesso)

Compromise me.
Compromise you.
Compromise this.
Compromise that.
Compromise friends.
Compromise friendship.
Compromise LO❤E.
Compromise Life.
Compromise Existence.
Compromise the World.
Compromise your HE❤Rt.
Compromise your Soul.
Compromise your Principles.
Compromise your integrity.
Compromise your Ideals.
Compromise your Values.
Compromise your politics.
Compromise your Religion.
Compromise your Spirituality.
Compromise is everywhere.
Compromise is everything.
Compromise is ALL.
Don't worry.
We're ALL Compromised
We ALL Compromise.

"The Don"
25.04.2021

Passion or Nothing
(Passione o Niente)

Unfortunately, Passion doesn't last.
Passion dies.
And what is left is...
...conformity.
...boredom
...the boring,
...the mundane,
...the routine,
...the obligation,
...the commitment,
...the emptiness,
...the loneliness,
...the ritual,
...fakeness.

Can one live a life always in passion?
Is this possible?
Or are we doomed to live a life of shallow, emptiness?

Inspired by the film "Swept Away... by an Unusual Destiny in the Blue Sea of August" (Italian: Travolti da un insolito destino nell'azzurro mare d'agostoby) by "Lina Wertmüller" (1974)

"The Don"
25.04.2021

The Siren

(la Sirena)

You hear her sing.
You hear her song.
You can't help but be entranced.
You can't help but be captivated.
You can't help but be captured.
You can't help but be trapped.
You can't help but be snared.
By....
....the Siren.

You are powerless.
You are helpless.
It's useless to struggle.
Once you have been dazzled by her song.
There is no point struggling.
There is no point fighting it.
Your will is no longer your own.
She controls your destiny.
You cannot resist.
You are trapped.
By....
....the Siren.

She will play with you.
She will tease you.
She will taunt you.
She will excite you.
She will arouse you.
She will hurt you.
She will do whatever she wants with & to you.
You are now her slave.
You are imprisoned.
By....
....*the Siren.*

There is no escape.
There is no way out.
There is no place to hide.
There is no place to run to.
There is nothing you can do.
Until she has had her way with you.
Until she no longer needs you.
Until you are no longer useful to her.
Then & only then, will you be set free.
By....
....*the Siren.*

"Resistance is futile!"

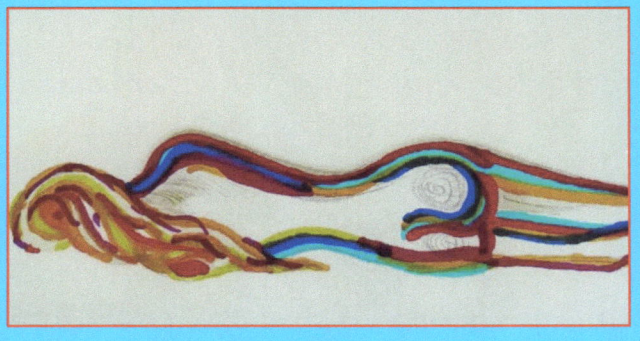

"The Don"
26.04.2021

Mas Turbation

(Mas Turbarsi)

Self-release.
Self-absorption.
Self-titillation.
Self-pleasure.
Self-pleasuring.
Self-gratification.
Self-eroticism.
Self-arousal.
Self-Lo♥e.

Do the *"hand-jive"*.
Why not *"tickle the Pink"*.
There ain't nothing wrong.
Everyone is doing it.
Self-satisfaction is the way to go.
Don't wait for someone else.
They don't know what to do.
They won't get it right.
Just do it yourself.
Get right every time.
It's the dance of *"Self-Lo♥e"*.
Do the *"Mas Turbation"* dance.

"Mas Turbation" is the way to go!
In fact, I feel like doing the *"Mas Turbation"* dance right now.
Why not join me?
We can *"Mas Turbation"* together.
Now, that would be FUN.
Let's ALL do the *"Mas Turbation"*!

"The Don"
26.04.2021

Reprocipity

(Riprocipità)

Maybe it's *"Karma"*?
It could be *"Ying & Yang"*.
Or maybe *"retribution"*.
Possibly *"atonement"*.
Or even, *Newton's 3rd Law of motion* is applicable.
"To every action there is an equal & opposite reaction"!
Or simply, *"what goes round comes round"*.
I call it *"Reprocipity"*!

"What you do unto others comes back to you".
It comes back & bites you on the bum!
So, watch out.
Take care!
Beware!
Your actions will return to you!
This is *"Reprocipity"*!

Sometimes you don't even mean to hurt people.
Sometimes you don't even know the consequences of your actions.
Sometimes you're just not aware.
Take *"LO♥E"* as an example.
Someone *"LO♥ES"* you but you don't share that feeling.
Alternatively, you *"LO♥E"* someone but they don't share that feeling.
Two sides of the same coin.
"Reprocipity"!

"It is what it is!"
That's all.
That is the nature of things.
That is Life.
And there's nothing you can do about it.
Just accept it & move on.
Doing as little damage as possible.
It's just *"Reprocipity"*!

"The Don"
27.04.2021

V for victory.
V for validictory.
V for victorious.
V for vain.
V for vanity.
V for volume.
V for voluminous.
V for Vanadium.
V for Valium
V for validity.
V for voice.
V for vocal.
V for view.
V for vice.
V for vexatious.
V for vaccination.
V for velocity.
V for vapping.
V for vagina.
V for V (5).
V for violence (NEVER).
V for V(P)eace.
V for Venice (the most beautiful city in the world).
V for Vito.

"The Don"
30.04.2021

I'm Arrogant

(Io Sono arrogante)

I know that I'm the best.
I know that I'm awesome.
I know that I'm number one.
I know that I'm unique.
I know that I'm irreplaceable.
I know that I'm smart.
I know that I'm intelligent.
I know that I'm intellectual.
I know that I'm creative.
I know that I'm a *"force of nature"*.
I know that I'm powerful.
I know that I'm forceful.
I know that I'm selfish.
I know that I'm self-centred.
I know that I'm a failure.
I know that I'm a loser.
I know that there's no one like me.
I know that the world revolves around me.
I know that the universe revolves around me.
I know that I'm arrogant.

Is that bad?

"The Don"
30.04.2021

Domesticated

(Addomesticata)

You're living with your boyfriend.
You're playing house.
You're pleasuring him in whatever way he wants.

You're cooking his dinner.
You're washing his underpants.
You become Domesticated.

You no longer go out to parties
You no longer rage all night.
You no longer drink copious amounts of beer.
You no longer smoke dope.
You just sit at home & watch *"Netflix"*.

You're cooking his dinner.
You're washing his underpants.
You become Domesticated.

You've lost your curiosity.
You're no longer interesting.
You tell the same *"old"* stories.
You have nothing new to say.
Because you do NOTHING!
You've become boring.

You're cooking his dinner.
You're washing his underpants.
You become Domesticated.

You're cooking his dinner.
You're washing his underpants.
You become Domesticated.

Anyway, have a good life!

"The Don"
01.05.2021

Compromise verses Benefits

(Vantaggi versetti Compromesso)

The Nature of relationships.

The mechanics & dynamics involved.
There are always compromises to be made.
But equally, there are always benefits to be gained.
If the benefits outweigh the compromises, you *stay*.
If the compromises outweigh the benefits, you *leave*.
It's always a balance between *compromise verses benefits.*

This is the formula.
This is the equation.
It's all quite simple.
That's the nature of relationships.
It's a balance between *compromise verses benefits.*

Which side are you leaning towards?

Compromise or benefits?

"The Don"
01.05.2021

Man....in Chaos

(Uomo ... nel Caos)

Man in *disorder*.
Man in *turmoil*.
Man in *confusion*.
Man *disarray*.

Man in *order*.
Man in *control*.
Man in *structure*.
Man in *array*.

Order verses *disorder*.
Which is better?
Order seems appealing.
Yet, it leads to Fascism & totalitarian regimes.
Disorder seems unappealing.
But it leads to social change & new ideas.

The choice is yours.
What do you prefer?
The "Era of Order"
Or...
The "Era of Chaos"

"I'll choose chaos over order every time!"

"Enjoy the chaos!"

"The Don"
02.05.2021

I Was Not a Good Friend

(Non ero un Buon Amico)

I was not a good friend that is true.
You told me that.
And after a lot of soul searching & self-reflection.
I agree!
I have realised that now.
I should have acted differently.
I should have behaved better.
You were right....
....when you said,
"I was not a good friend".

I was jealous.
I misread the situation.
I overreacted.
I acted rashly.
I acted impulsively.
I acted stupidly.
I was an idiot.
I was a fool.
You were right...
....when you said,
"I was not a good friend".

I have reflected a lot on this.
I have thought about it often.
I have learned a lot since then.
I have made mistakes...
...that is true.
...I accept that.
But you were right...
....when you said,
"I was not a good friend".

"I was NOT a good friend!"

The Don"
04.05.2021

How Young Are You?
(Quanto Giovane se tu?)

That is how your age should be asked.
How young are you?
Not...
....how old are you?
Don't ask, *"How old are you?"*
Ask, *"How young are you?"*, instead.

Let's change the question.
Let's redefine age.
Let's focus on *"young"*.
Let's not focus on *"old"*.
Don't ask, *"How old are you?"*
Ask, *"How young are you?"*, instead.

Maintain your youth.
Maintain your *"inner child"*.
Maintain your innocence.
Maintain your curiosity.
Maintain your questioning.
Don't ask, *"How old are you?"*
Ask, *"How young are you?"*, instead.

"How young are you?"

"The Don"
06.05.2021

Faceless

(Senza Faccia)

I have no face.
I have no personality.
I have no identity.
I have no persona
I have no voice.
I have no eyes.
I have no mouth.
I have no mind.
I have no individuality.
I am faceless.

I don't feel.
I don't see.
I don't hear.
I don't feel
I don't exist.
I don't live.
I am faceless.

No point trying.
No point complaining.
No point crying.
No point denying.
No point lying
I am faceless.

"The Don"
07.05.2021

Women Have the Power
(Le Donne hanno il Potere)

Don't complain.
Don't argue.
Don't fight it.
Don't struggle.
Woman have the POWER.

They pull the strings.
They decide.
They control.
They say yes or no.
Woman have the POWER.

There is nothing you can do about it.
There is no point in fighting it.
There is no point in arguing.
There is point in struggling.
Woman have the POWER.

They either want you or they don't.
They either like you or they don't.
They either LO♥E you or they don't.
They either will FUCK you or they won't.
Woman have the POWER.

"The Don"
07.05 2021

You Can't Go Back

(Non Puoi Tornare Indietro)

No, you can't.
No matter how much you try.
No matter how much you will it.
No matter how much you wish for it.
No matter how much you pray for it.
No matter how much you would die for it.
You can't go back!

What is done, is done.
It cannot be undone.
It cannot be rewritten.
It cannot be erased.
It cannot be removed.
It is written in stone.
Because you can't go back!

You can cry.
You can be sad.
You can moan.
You can be angry.
You can become religious.
You can turn to God.
But.....
....you can't go back!

No matter what you do...
....you can't go back!

You can only go forward.
Because....
....you can't go back!

"The Don"
08.05.2021

The Creative Process
(Il Processo Creativo)

Don't think.
Don't overthink.
Don't hesitate.
Don't procrastinate.
Don't doubt.
Don't block.
Don't stop.
Just do it!
This is the "Creative Process".

Listen to your HE❤RT.
Listen to your SOUL.
Listen to you guts.
Listen to your inside.
Listen to your Energy.
Just....
....do it.
This is the "Creative Process".

Don't listen to your *HEAD*.
Don't listen to what others think.
Don't listen to what others say.
Don't listen to what others feel.
Don't listen to the downers.
Don't listen to the negatives.
Don't listen to those that say *"you can't"*!
Just....
....do it.
This is the "Creative Process".

Just....
....let the energy flow.
....let the mind be free.
....let your HE♥RT be free.
....let your HE♥RT explode.
....let your being fly.
....let yourself go crazy.
....let yourself become energy.
....let yourself become *"one"* with the Universe.
Just....
....do it.
This is the "Creative Process".

Inspired by Mike whom I met "Sappho Bar", Glebe

"The Don"
08.05.2021

Are You Happy?

(Sei Felice?)

Are you content?
Are you joyful?
Are you enjoying your life?
Are you doing what you want to do?
Are you at peace with yourself?
Are you happy?

Have you made too many compromises?
Have you traded away too much?
Have you lost yourself?
Have you lost your way?
Are you happy?

Happiness is a state of mind.
Happiness is illusory.
Happiness is an *"internal"* state.
Happiness is *"peace of mind"*.
Happiness is contagious.
Are you happy?

Are you happy with your life?
Are you happy?
I mean.....
Are you REALLY happy?

"The Don"
08.05.2021

Sex is NOT LO♥E

(Il Sesso NON è Amore)

Sex is physical.
Sex is mechanical.
Sex is impersonal.
Sex is unemotional.
Sex is empty.
Sex is ex-clusive.
Sex is unfulfilling.
Sex lacks intimacy.
Sex lacks connection.
Sex lacks empathy.
Sex can be bought.
Sex is objectification.
Sex is NOT LO♥E.

LO♥E is personal.
LO♥E is a connection.
LO♥E is communication.
LO♥E is in-clusive.
LO♥E is intimacy.
LO♥E is emotional.
LO♥E is fulfilling.
LO♥E is healing.
LO♥E is Spiritual.
LO♥E is NOT fake.
LO♥E CANNOT be bought.
Sex is NOT LO♥E.

"The Don"
08.05.2021

Relationships

(Relazioni)

Relationships are complicated creatures.
Relationships are never simple.
Relationships are never easy.
Relationships are fraught with difficulties.
Relationships are a minefield to manoeuvre.
Relationships are tumultuous.
Relationships are like sailing stormy waters.
Relationships are painful.
Relationships are full of suffering.
Relationships are a nightmare.
Relationships are horrendous.
Relationships are uncharted territory.
Relationships are unpredictable.
Relationships are full of unimaginable obstacles.
Relationships are necessary.
Relationships are unavoidable.
Relationships are part of life.
Relationships are inescapable.
Relationships are an intrinsic part of living.
Relationships are hard work.
Relationships are beautiful (sometimes).

"The Don"
10.05.2021

Good Things Come to those that Wait
(Le Cose Buone Arrivano a Coloro che Aspettano)

Be patient.
Be calm.
Be resolute.
Be strong.
Be at peace.
Be free.
Good things come to those that wait.

Don't be impatient.
Don't be needy.
Don't be greedy.
Don't be stressed.
Don't be agitated.
Don't think a lot
Good things come to those that wait.

Take your time.
Smell the roses.
Live in the moment.
Let it be.
Meditate.
Stay focused.
Good things come to those that wait.

But the waiting is the hardest part!

"The Don"
10.05.2021

Creative Disorder

(Disordine Creativo)

Let chaos rule supreme.
Let disorder be the norm.
Let's break all the laws.
Let's get rid of all the rules.
Let there be "Creative Disorder".

I don't like order.
I don't like rules.
I don't like laws.
I don't like the police.
I don't like politicians.
I don't like Fascists.
I don't like Fascism.
Let's have "Creative Disorder" instead.

I like chaos.
I like disorder.
I like anarchy.
I like anarchists.
I like FREEDOM.
I like "Creative Disorder"

"Order is imposed from above."
"It distorts, frustrates, discourages & stops creativity!"
"I also feel that rules are made to be broken, especially in art!"
"I prefer creative disorder to strict rules."
- *"Lina Wertmüller"*

Inspired by "Lina Wertmüller" the FIRST WOMAN to be nominated for an Oscar for best director in 1977 for the film "7 Beauties" (Pasqualino Settebellezze)!

"The Don"
10.05.2021

Make Me Happy

(Rendermi Felice)

(This is based on a "WhatsApp" conversation with a complete stranger)

Hi BEAUTIFUL!

Good.

I'm TERRIFIC! How are you doing?

How was your night last night?

Nothing special. How was yours?

Cool.

Where are you from dear?
I am from Germany DE.
And I am 37 years single.

My name is Vito
I'm from Sydney Australia

Cool
What did you do for work?
And how old are you?
You look handsome.
My dear, I am *Jii Hardener* by name.

Hi Jii, you are SuPeR SEXY!!!

Really

I'm a poet!

I am looking for a man who will make me happy and be there for me always.

That is not me!
I live "in the moment"!
I LO❤️*E people too much!*
Especially SEXY, HOT babes like yourself!

That's cool.
Will you make me happy dear?
And I will also make sure I surprise you.

❤️❤️❤️❤️❤️❤️❤️❤️

Unfortunately, no to that as well!
You can only make yourself happy!!!
I can't make you happy!!!

That's bad.

Happiness comes from within you!

I can't take that dear.

I know, it's hard to accept!

Yes.

I wanted someone else to make me happy but I realised that I have to make myself happy!!!
You don't need me or anybody else to make you happy!
You are so beautiful, believe in yourself!

Yes, you make me happy, I can make you happy.

Sorry!
Like I said, I can't make you happy & you can't make me happy!
I wish I could.
"External" happiness is transitory.
"Internal" happiness is permanent.
"External" objects provide only "provisional" happiness.
"Internal" qualities create a "permanent state of happiness".
I'm "external".
I can only provide you with a "provisional state of happiness".

"The Don"
13.05.2021

Don't Sweat the Small Stuff
(Non Sudare le Piccole Cose)

Work out what's important for yourself.
Prioritise your needs.
Make a list from most important to least important.
Stick to this list.
Don't sweat the small stuff.

You don't have to fight every situation.
Ask yourself, *"Is this so important?"*
"Do I have to put all my energy into this?"
"Do I need to fight for this?"
Because don't sweat the small stuff.

Choose your battles wisely.
Look at the *"bigger"* picture.
Step back from the immediate situation.
Ask yourself, *"Is this really important?"*
"Is it worth fighting over?"
"Or are their more important issues for me to save my battles for?"
Don't sweat the small stuff.

The minutiae, is not worth fighting over.
The day-to-day boring struggles are not that important.
Save your battles for the big issues.
Store your energy for when you will really need it.
For those situations that really require & demand it.
But please, don't sweat the small stuff.

It's really not worth it.
And to be honest, it's just a waste of time & energy.
So, don't sweat the small stuff.
Whatever you do...
...don't sweat the small stuff.

"The Don"
13.05.2021

I Don't Believe in Anything

(Io Non Credo a Niente)

I don't believe in *me*.
I don't believe *you*.
I don't believe in *politicians*.
I don't believe in *politics*.
I don't believe in *society*.
I don't believe in *religion*.
I don't believe in *religions*.
I don't be in *God*.
I don't believe in the *Devil*.
I don't believe in *you*.
I don't believe in anything.

I don't believe in *Capitalism*.
I don't believe in *Communism*.
I don't believe in *Socialism*.
I don't believe in *The State*.
I don't believe in the *Universe*.
I don't believe in *existence*.
I don't believe in anything.

I don't believe in *Hate*.
I don't believe in the *HE♥RT*.
I don't believe in the *Soul*.
I don't believe in *LO♥E*.
I don't believe in anything.

I don't believe *you*.
I don't believe in *me*.
I don't believe in anything.

"I don't believe in anything!"
That's what I believe in!

"But have a good life anyway!"

"The Don"
13.05.2021

Ska8er Girl

(Ragazza Ska8er)

She's always on the move.
She also likes to groove.
She's my ska8er Girl.

She's likes to have fun.
She's always on the run.
My ska8er Girl.

She works in a bar.
She doesn't live very far.
My ska8er Girl.

She's works at *"Sappho Bar"*.
She's doesn't need a car.
My ska8er Girl.

She says she writes poems.
But no one even knows thems.
My ska8er Girl.

I told her to, *"Publish books"*.
"It's not as hard as it looks".
My ska8er Girl.

She said, *"Maybe I should"*.
I said, *"I hope you would"*.
My ska8er Girl.

She's an alright gal.
I think she's my pal.
My ska8er Girl.

I gave her my book.
She said *"You really cook"*.
My ska8er Girl.

Her name is *"Bella"*.
She gonna be a *"stella"*.
My ska8er Girl.

I said *"If I can do it, Bella"*.
"You can do it as wella".
My ska8er Girl.

She's works at *"Sappho Bar"*.
She's gonna go far.
My ska8er Girl.

(Inspired by a real life "ska8er Girl", "Bella", who actually works at "Sappho Bar", Glebe.)

"Skate, skate, skater girl!
1, 2, 3, Let`s go!
Baby take your rollerblades, come with me to town
Let`s go the street up, let`s go it down
Baby we can go to the beach and take a swim
You`ve got nothing to lose but a whole lot to win
Oh yeah, hee-ey"

Written by: AGELII-LESKELA, LJUNG Performed by "Shebang"

"The Don"
15.05.2021

Feelin' Groovy

(Sensazione di Groovy)

Speed up you're moving too slow.
You gotta let the morning go.
Just running down the cobblestones.
Having fun & feelin' groovy,
I'm feelin' groovy.
Feelin'groovy.

Goodbye goalpost, what'cha showin'?
I don't have time to watch your flowers growin'.
Don't need no rhymes from you today.
All is groovy.
I'm feelin' groovy.
Feelin'groovy.

I've got a lot of deeds to do, plenty of promises to keep.
I'm rocking 'n rolling, no time to sleep.
Don't let the morning time drop its minutes on me.
Life, I have no love for you today,
Don't hold me back get outta my way
All is groovy.
I'm feelin' groovy.
Feelin'groovy.

Having fun & feelin' groovy,
I'm feelin' groovy.
Feelin'groovy.

"Thanks to "The 59th Street Bridge Song",
"Sung by Simon & Garfunkel, written by Paul Simon"

"The Don"
15.05.2021

Mas Turbation

(Mas Turbarsi)

Self-release.
Self-absorption.
Self-titillation.
Self-pleasure.
Self-pleasuring.
Self-gratification.
Self-eroticism.
Self-arousal.
Self-Lo♥e.
It's "Mas Turbation" time.

Do the "hand-jive".
Why not "tickle the Pink".
There ain't nothing wrong.
Everyone is doing it.
Self-satisfaction is the way to go.
Don't wait for someone else.
They don't know what to do.
They won't get it right.
Just do it yourself.
Get right every time.
It's the dance of "Self-Lo♥e".
Do the "Mas Turbation" dance.

"The Don"
26.04.2021

Lo♥e is a Commodity

(L'amore è una Merce)

Lo♥e is bought & sold.
Lo♥e is a piece of merchandise.
Lo♥e is a consumer item.
Lo♥e is a disposable object.
Lo♥e is a commodity.

What price have you put on your Lo♥e?
How much have you sold your Lo♥e for?
What have you sold your Lo♥e for?
Did you get a good price?
Because Lo♥e is a commodity.

Did you sell your Lo♥e for...
...money?
...marriage?
...children?
...sex?
...fame?
...fortune?
...security?
...friendship?
...a career?
...a "nerdy" Australian man?
...an Australian visa?
Because Lo♥e is a commodity.

I hope you're happy with your deal.
I hope you're happy with your purchase.
I hope you're happy with your life.
I hope you're satisfied with your sale.
Because Lo♥e is a commodity.

"The Don"
17.05.2021

I Live in My Head

(Vivo Nella Mia Testa)

My head is my home.
I never leave it.
I never go out.
I do whatever I want here.
There are no rules.
There are no laws.
The laws of Physics don't apply in here.
I live in my head.

It's my world.
It's my *"Reality"*.
It's my *"Fantasy"*.
It's my *"Universe"*.
It's my *"Friend"*.
It's my *"Enemy"*.
It's my *"Lo❤er"*.
It's my *"Destroyer"*.
I live in my head.

In here....
I am *God*.
I am the *Devil*.
I am a *saint*.
I am a *sinner*.
I am *"good"*.
I am "bad".
I am *honest*.
I am a *liar*.
I live in my head.

I am a prisoner.
I cannot leave.
I can NEVER leave.
I am trapped.
I cannot escape.
I cannot get out.
I can NEVER be free.
I can NEVER be released.
I am doomed to live in here FOREVER.
I live in my head.

I want to leave!
But I cannot!
Someone please, help me.
Someone please come & rescue me.
Someone please come & blow up this prison.
Someone please set me free.
I will pay you well.
But I don't have any money.
I can only pay you in kindness.
I live in my head.

I didn't want to live in here.
I didn't choose to live in here.
I had no choice.
I HAVE no choice.
I was born in here.
I've lived my whole life in here.
I will die in here.
I live in my head.

I am punished in here.
I am tormented & tortured by my thoughts.
My memories, they haunt me.
My dreams, they tantalise me.
They are relentless.
They are merciless.
They never stop.
It's cruel & unusual punishment.
It's a constant bombardment.
I live in my head.

It's a very bad place.
I don't want to live here anymore.
I don't want to live in my head.

It's such a lonely place!

"The Don"
20.05.2021

Do Not Think

(Non Pensare)

Stop thinking.
Stop your thoughts.
Stop the noise in your brain.
Shut your brain down.
Turn your brain off.
Do not think.

Thinking causes stress.
Thinking causes neurosis.
Thinking causes cancer.
Thinking kills!
Turn your brain off.
Do not think.

Thinking causes *"overthinking"*.
"Overthinking" causes a nervous breakdown.
Stop thinking.
Stop your thoughts.
Stop the noise in your brain.
Shut your brain down.
Turn your brain off.
Do not think.

You will live longer.
You will be happier.
Stop thinking.
Stop your thoughts.
Stop the noise in your brain.
Shut your brain down.
Turn your brain off.
Do not think.

Thinking is bad for your physical health.
Thinking is bad for your mental health.
Stop thinking.
Stop your thoughts.
Stop the noise in your brain.
Shut your brain down.
Turn your brain off.
Do not think.

Whatever you do, "Do not think!"

"The Don"
20.05.2021

Miriam is Dead

(Miriam è Morta)

She never really existed.
She was just a figment of my imagination.
Miriam is dead.

She was an *illusion*.
She was a *delusion*.
She was a *fantasy*.
She was a *dream*.
She was a *nightmare*.
She drove me *crazy*.
She drove me *insane*.
She drove me *mad*.
She drove me to *madness*.
She drove me *wild*.
She had me under her spell.
But now, Miriam is dead.

May she "rest in peace".
May I "rest in peace".
May I overcome her spell.
May I break free from her chains.
May I never think of her ever again.
May I move on & never look back.
May I stop looking for her on the streets.
May I stop wanting to bump into her at a bar.
May I stop thinking about her 24/7.
Because Miriam is dead.

Yes, Miriam is dead.

It was an excruciatingly slow death.
She did not want to die.
She fought hard.
She struggled against it.
She put up an extremely good fight.
She is definitely is a survivor *(I can tell you that)*.
But she finally succumbed to the inevitable…..
….her death.
Miriam is dead.

She has been exorcised from my *"Being"*.
She has been removed from my *"Soul"*.
She has been wrenched from my HE♥RT.
She is no longer inside of me.
She has departed my consciousness.
She is no longer my *tormentor*.
She is no longer my *"Mistress"*.
She is no longer my "Enslaver"
I am no longer her *"slave"*.
I am no longer *"enslaved"*.
I am finally FREE.
Miriam is dead.

Let's have a party!
Let's celebrate!
The death of Miriam.
For finally……
Miriam is dead!

"Drinks all round!"
"Miriam is dead!"

"Psychologically speaking, of course!"

"The Don"
20.05.2021

I am the Tit Man

(Io sono il Tit Uomo)

I LOVE breasts.
I LOVE boobs.
I LOVE boobies.
I LOVE tits.
I LOVE titties.
I LOVE nipples.
I LOVE looking at breasts.
I LOVE touching breasts.
I LOVE cuddling breasts.
I LOVE stroking breasts.
I LOVE kissing breasts.
I LOVE licking breasts.
I LOVE sucking breasts.
I LOVE biting breasts.
I LOVE breasts.

I am the "Breast Man"!
I am the "Tit Man".

"Is the something wrong with that?"
"Is there something wrong with me?"

"The Don"
29.05.2021

I am a WOG: WOG Boy

I am not a native of this land.
I was not born here.
I was born in another place & time.
I was born in Southern Italy.
I am a WOG Boy.

I am an immigrant.
I had no choice in the matter.
I was not asked if I wanted to come here.
I was brought out with my mother & brother.
I am a WOG Boy.

I came out on a huge ocean liner.
It was called *"The Galileo"*.
I'd never seen an ocean before.
I'd never seen a boat before.
I am a WOG Boy.

I was 5 years young.
I came from a farm in southern Italy.
We were poor.
There was very little food.
I am a WOG Boy.

I was a happy.
I played with my cousins.
I played with my faithful companion, *"Sargento"*.
He was my protector, my guardian, my friend, my dog.
I am a WOG Boy.

I had a happy childhood.
Until I was 5 years young.
Then I was brought to another country.
I was transplanted to *"Terra Australis"*, Australia.
I am a WOG Boy.

It was December 1964.
When I set foot in another country.
This country known as the *"Great Southern Land"*.
"The land of hope & opportunity".
I am a WOG Boy.

My life changed forever.
I was a curly, redheaded, freckled skinned boy from a foreign land.
I ate different food.
Spoke a different language.
I had a weird name...
Vito...
Radice...
"WTF sorta name is that?"
Many times, I wanted to change my name.
(In fact, I did once. I called myself Victor. Bad move. It didn't work out well. But I digress, that's another story).
I wore different clothes.
I sang different songs.
I had a different culture.
I was not from here.
I was not accepted.
I was pantsed.
I was taunted.
I was bullied
I was laughed at.
I was ridiculed.
I was humiliated.
I felt ashamed.
I cried.
I was alone.
I was sad.
I was not happy.
I did not fit in.
I did not want to be who I was.
I wanted to be an *"Aussie"!*
But.....
.....*I was a WOG Boy.*

I am a WOG!

"I am a WOG & I am proud!"
"I'm a WOG BOY!"
"Shout it out LOUD!"
"I'm a WOG BOY!"
"& I am proud!"
"I'm a WOG BOY!"

"I am a WOG!"

"WOG" was a derogatory, racist word used to put down immigrants from southern Europe during the 40s, 50s, 60s & 70s in Australia under the "White Australia Policy". It is now a "badge of honour"!

"The Don"
21.05.2021

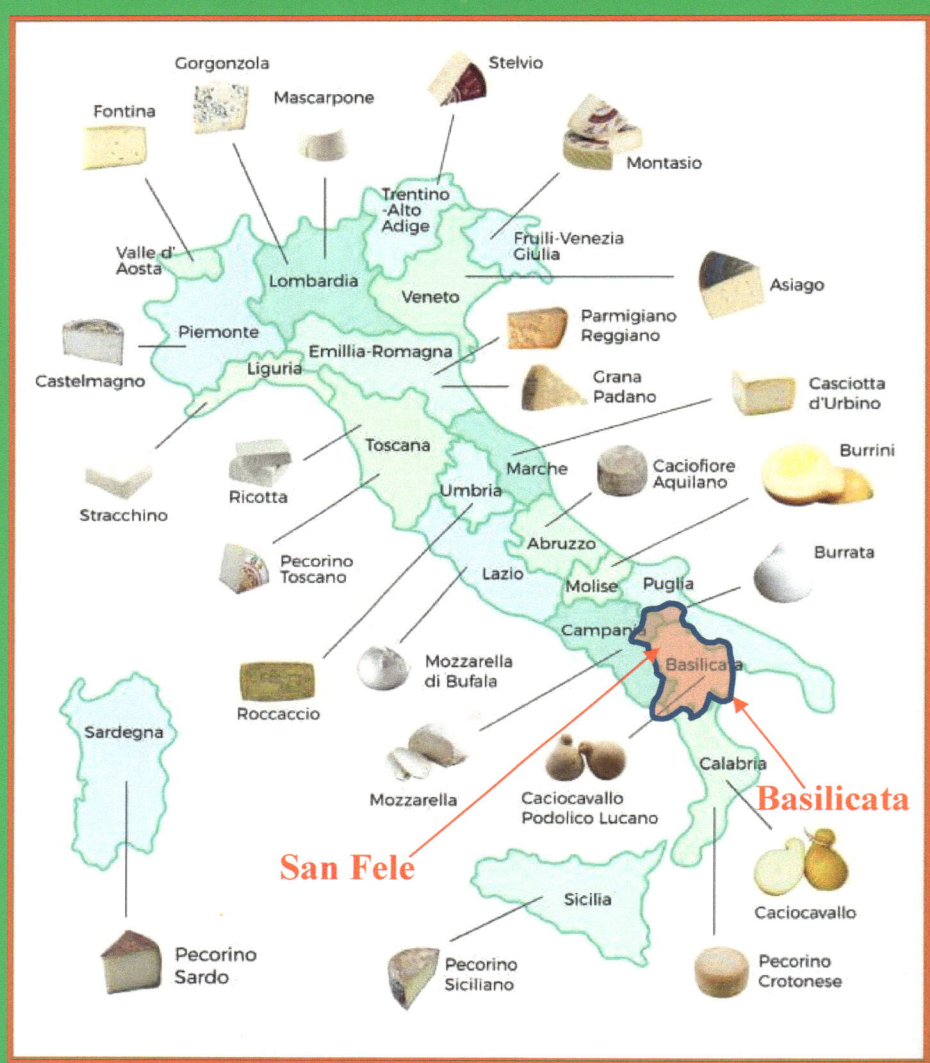

I was born in a small village called *"San Fele"*, in the region of Italy called *"Basilicata"*.

Clothing Maketh the Man
(Vestiti Fa L'uomo)

Or is it..
The man maketh the clothing?
Is it what you wear that describes you?
Or is it..
What you are that describes what you wear?

I feel good when I wear nice clothing.
Well made, stylish.
I stand taller.
I feel proud of myself.
Is this vanity?
I am vain?
Maybe, it's the Italian in me?
It is well known that Italians are very stylish!

I like to look good.
I like to look stylish.
At least to myself.
That's all that really matters anyway.
That's the only thing that counts.
How I feel about myself!

I like it, of course, if someone says,
"Hey, you look very dapper!"
Who wouldn't?
It's always a nice feeling when a stranger pays you a compliment.
Something unexpected.
Someone unknown.
So, does...
The man maketh the clothing?
Or...
The clothing maketh the man?

"The Don"
21.05.2021

Scars

(Cicatrici)

We all have scars.
We have all been scared.
We all carry our scars with us.
Throughout our entire lives.
All these scars may not have healed.
They still impinge on us.
They affect us.
These scars maybe physical.
These scars maybe psychology....
...mental scars.
Scars in our mind.
These are the worst sorts of scars.
Because unlike the physical ones, they can't be seen.
They're not as easily repaired.
They're not as easily healed.
We all carry scars.

These scars are caused from wounds.
Deep psychology wounds.
Wounds that one has accumulated over an entire lifetime.
Wounds that have been inflicted upon us by others.
Wounds that we have inflicted upon ourselves.
Some, if not many of these wounds, are still *"weeping"* today.....
.....many years later.
They have not *healed*.
They are still *"raw"*.
They are still *"sour"*.
They are still *"bleeding"*.
They are still *"weeping"*.
Maybe, many years later.
They have NEVER formed scars.

Some of these wounds run deep.
Some of these wounds have NEVER healed.
How many wounds do you have?
How many are still not healed?
How many scars do you have?
I hope it's not too many.
I hope you one of the *"lucky"* ones.
One that hasn't been wounded severely.
One that doesn't have too many scars.

This is life....
The accumulation of wounds & scars.

"How many wounds & scars have you accumulated?"
"I hope it's not too many."

I am one of those *"lucky"* ones.

"The Don"
22.05.2021

Rejection revisited

(Rigetto rivisitato)

Rejection.....
....always hurts a little bit.
No matter how much you pretend it doesn't.
There is always something that penetrates your armour.
There is always a chink in it.
You cannot deny it....
You have been rejected.

You try to shrug it off.
You try to be brave.
You try to be cool.
You try to be tough.
You try to brush it off
But it's always hard to deal with...
... rejection.

You try to intellectualise the situation.
You try to rationalise it away.
You try to move on as though nothing has happened.
You try to deny...
....that you have been...
.... rejected.

Rejection is a lonely feeling.
Rejection is a lonely place.
Rejection makes you retreat back into yourself.
Rejection always leaves one feeling empty inside.
Rejection is something I know only too well.
Rejection is my friend.
I know rejection well.
It's nothing new to me.
Don't worry...
.... it's just rejection again.

Get over it!

"The Don"
22.05.2021

A Poem for Bob

(Una Poesia per Bob)

How many roads have you travelled, Bob?
How many seas have you crossed!
How many songs have you written?
How many lovers have you had?

Tell me, how does it feel, Bob?
To be on your own?
With no direction home?
A complete unknown?
Like a rolling stone?

How many lives have you lived, Bob?
How many songs have you sung!
How many times have the times changed?
How often have you been love sick?
How many times have you been sick of love?

Well, the answer Bob,
Is blowing in the wind.
The answer, is blowing in the wind.

Tell me, how does it feel, Bob?
To be on your own?
With no direction home?
A complete unknown?
Like a rolling stone?

How many times be along the watchtower, Bob?
How many times have you slept on the sand?
How many times have you sung "Mr Tambourine Man"?
How many ears must a man have, Bob, before he can hear peoples' cries?

Well, the answer Bob,
Is blowing in the wind.
The answer, is blowing in the wind.

Tell me, how does it feel, Bob?
To be on your own?
With no direction home?
A complete unknown?
Like a rolling stone?

Have the times really changed, Bob?
The Masters' still have all the guns.
They still have all the bombs.
And they still have blood in their veins.
But, yes Bob, there is blood on the tracks.
And I do have desire!
But where is the man in black, Bob?
Where is he when we need him the most?

Well, the answer Bob,
Is blowing in the wind.
The answer, is blowing in the wind.

Tell me, how does it feel, Bob?
To be on your own?
With no direction home?
A complete unknown?
Like a rolling stone?

Anyway Bob, happy 80th birthday!

You're a legend!

(Dedicated to Bob Dylan (Robert Zimmerman), born 24.05.1941)

"How many roads must a man walk down
Before you call him a man?
How many seas must a white dove sail
Before she sleeps in the sand?
Yes, and how many times must the cannonballs fly
Before they're forever banned?

The answer, my friend, is blowin' in the wind
The answer is blowin' in the wind

Yes, and how many years must a mountain exist
Before it is washed to the sea?
And how many years can some people exist
Before they're allowed to be free?
Yes, and how many times can a man turn his head
And pretend that he just doesn't see?

The answer, my friend, is blowin' in the wind
The answer is blowin' in the wind

Yes, and how many times must a man look up
Before he can see the sky?
And how many ears must one man have
Before he can hear people cry?
Yes, and how many deaths will it take 'til he knows
That too many people have died?

The answer, my friend, is blowin' in the wind
The answer is blowin' in the wind."

Songwriter: Bob Dylan

'The Don"
24.05.2021

The Only Thing We've Got Left is Sophistication
(L'unica cosa che ci Resta è la Sofisticazione)

Stand tall.
Walk proud.
Wear it well.
Be slick.
Look slick.
Be stylish.
This is the only thing you've got left.
Make it work for you.
Otherwise, you're just a part of the woodwork.
You're just wallpaper.
You're invisible.
The only thing that you've got left is SOPHISTICATION.

Our youth is gone.
Our looks have disappeared.
Our hair has fallen.
Our gut has grown.
Our skin is flabby.
Our knees are wobbly.
Our face had drooped.
Our eyes have bags.
Our jowls have dropped.
Gravity has worn us down.
But.....
The only thing that you've got left is SOPHISTICATION.

Let this work for you.
Stand out from the rest.
Stand out from the crowd.
Walk out of the woodwork.
Step out of the wallpaper!
You have what others don't.
You might be old (physically)....
....but....
...you have something they don't....
....*SOPHISTICATION.*

"At our age, the only thing that we've got left is SOPHISTICATION".

(From a conversation with, inspired & dedicated to my BEST friend & a true bro, Greg)

"The Don"
24.05.2021

Life is a Bummer, Sometimes
(La Vita è una Peccata, a Volte)

Life is not all sunshine & roses.
Life is not a bouquet of flowers.
Life is not a box of chocolates.
Life is full of...
...ups & downs,
...straight roads & round-a-bouts.
...high roads & low roads
...winding narrow paths.
...treacherous seas.
...hurricanes a-blowing,
...times always a-changin',
...fortunes won & fortunes lost.
...Lo❤e won & Lo❤e lost.
Life is a bummer, sometimes!

Life is not all peaches & cream...
...Strawberries & cream,
...Ice cream,
Sometimes, there is no cream at all.
There's just a rock cake...
...stale bread,
...cheap wine,
...raw onions,
...porridge,
...bangers & mash (without tomato sauce or the peas),
You've just gotta accept that....
...Life is a bummer, sometimes!

(Inspired from a conversation with my good friend Vanessa)

"The Don"
25.05.2021

The Running Woman
(La Donna che Corre)

Where are you running to?
Whom are you running from?
How many roads have you run?
How many kilometres have you travelled?
How many are you gonna run?
When will your running stop?
Will you ever stop?

Running Woman stop for a while.
Running Woman stay for a while.
Running Woman stay the night.
Running Woman, you can start your running again in the morning.
Running Woman, you won't be late.
Running Woman stay with me.
Running Woman when was the last time you made LO♥E?
Running Woman don't go.
Running Woman don't run past me.
Running Woman stop for a rest.
Running Woman, will your running ever come to an end?
Running Woman, will I ever see you again?
Running Woman, will you ever run this way again?

Maybe, never.

Goodbye *Running Woman*!
Run well!

"Traveling lady, stay awhile,
Until the night is over.
I'm just a station on your way,
I know I'm not your lover."

Songwriter: Leonard Cohen

"The Don"
25.05.2021

I Am Responsible

(Io Sono Responsabile)

I am responsible for my own suffering.
I am responsible for my own sadness.
I am responsible for my own sorrow.
I am responsible for my own mistakes.
I am responsible for my own failures.
I am responsible for my own loses.
I am responsible for my own defeats.
I am responsible for my own inadequacies.
I am responsible for my own misinterpretations.
I am responsible for my own delusions.
I am responsible for my own illusions.
I am responsible for my own failings.
I am responsible for my own rejections.
I am responsible for my own short comings.
I am responsible for my own weaknesses.
I am responsible for my own actions.
I take full responsibility.
I am responsible.

I am to blame.
No one else.
Just me & me alone.
I am responsible.

"The Don"
25.05.2021

Be Yourself

(Essere te Stesso)

"Be Yourself", that's what they say.
But what the fuck does that actually mean?
"Be Yourself!"
Of course, who else can I be?
I can imitate.
I can copy,
I can impersonate,
I can mimic.
But regardless I am still *"Myself"*.
I can never be anyone else.
I can never be you, for example.
No matter how I try.
I can never be you!
I can only be "Myself".

The problem I have though is...
...who am I?
I really don't know who I am.
I am confused.
I am searching.
I am looking for myself.
Because I don't really know who I am.
Not really.
I pretend.
I bluff.
I fake.
I postulate.
I pontificate.
But who am I, really?
So that I can be "Myself".

Have you really found yourself?
Have you discovered who you are?
Have you worked what you are meant to be?
So that you can "Be Yourself"!

In my case, it has taken 61 years to finally find out who I am.
So, it's never too late.
Never give up!
Keep searching!
You might be as lucky as me.
To find out who you truly are.
So that finally you can "Be Yourself".

I am a poet!

Don"
26.05.2021

Abused

(Abusata)

If you FEEL that you've been abused,
Then you HAVE been abused.
It's that simple.
There is no argument to be had.
No conversation about intent or intention.
There is no compromising this fact.
If you feel you have been abused…
…you have been abused!

Of course, this statement is conditional.
Based on the proviso that….
One has to be honest.
One has to be truthful.
It should not be a lie.
It should not be an act of revenge.
An act of spite.
An act of vindictiveness.
An act of vexatious harm...
...to another person.

So, if a person honestly feels abused….
.. then they have been abused.
No matter the situation.
There are no excuses.
There are no reasons.
There are no justifications.
If you feel abused...
...then you have been abused.

It's a simple as that!

"The Don"
26.05.2021

Toxic Positivity

(Positività Tossica)

A new term I saw today.
"Toxic Positivity".
It started me thinking...
...this term suggests a state in which there is too much...
...positivity.
...kindness.
...caring.
...happiness.
...joy.
...FUN.
Can this ever be the case?
Can one ever get too much positivity?
Can one ever have too much positivity?
Does *"Toxic Positivity"* exist?

I have been told that I am too kind.
I have been told that I'm too easy.
I have been told that my kindness is an act of *"manipulation"*.
"Stop manipulating me!", I was told *(in no uncertain terms)*.
Does it really matter the intention of the act?
Isn't the act itself the only thing that matters?
"ACTIONS speak louder than WORDS!"
The fact is that the ACT is a *"positive"* act.

Can one ever GET too much positivity?
Can on ever HAVE too much positivity?
Does *"Toxic Positivity"* exist?

Isn't it better to have *"Toxic Positivity"* rather than no positivity at all?
Or to have hatred, abuse & violence instead?

Can one ever GET too much positivity?
Can on ever HAVE too much positivity?
Does *"Toxic Positivity"* exist?

"The Don"
27.05.2021

Superstition

(Superstizione)

Are you superstitious?
Do you believe in superstition?
Do believe that objects have power?
Do you believe that objects have power over you?
That they can control you?
Make you do things you don't want to do?

Do you believe that walking under a ladder brings you bad luck?
Do you believe that the number 13, 4 brings you bad luck?
Do you believe that if a black cat crosses your bath, you will have bad luck?
Having a rabbit's foot is superstitious *(poor rabbit only having 3 feet)*?
Broken mirrors giving you 7 years of *"bad"* luck?
Worshipping a statue is superstitious.
Religions are full of superstitious beliefs.
In fact, superstition is rampant throughout different societies & cultures.

...Witchcraft,
...Voodoo,
...Tarot cards,
...Crystals,
...astrology,
...Ouija boards,
...séances,
...wedding rings,
...rituals,
...ceremonies,
...supernatural experiences,
...paranormal phenomenae.

Are all superstitions, or involve a superstition mentality.

This is called *"Magical Consciousness"*.
Giving objects powers that they do not possess.
This is very commonly mistaken or confused as a *"Higher level of consciousness"*.
In fact, it is the exact opposite.
It is a *"Lower level of Consciousness"!*
In between the sleep & awaken states.
At the level of daydreams & reveries.

Are you a superstitious person?
Do you believe in superstition?

"Very superstitious,
Writing's on the wall,
Very superstitious,
Ladders bout' to fall,
Thirteen month old baby,
Broke the lookin' glass
Seven years of bad luck,
The good things in your past

When you believe in things
That you don't understand,
Then you suffer,
Superstition aint the way
Hey

Very superstitious,
Wash your face and hands,
Rid me of the problem,
Do all that you can,
Keep me in a daydream,
Keep me goin' strong,
You don't wanna save me,
Sad is the soul

When you believe in things
That you don't understand,
Then you suffer,
Superstition ain't the way,
Yeh, yeh

Very superstitious,
Nothin' more to say,
Very superstitious,
The devil's on his way,
Thirteen month old baby,
Broke the lookin' glass,
Seven years of bad luck,
Good things in your past

When you believe in things
That you don't understand,
Then you suffer,
Superstition ain't the way,
No, no, no."

Songwriter: Wonder Stevie

"The Don"
27.05.2021

Are You Happy #2?
(Sei Felice #2?)

Living in you little cocoon.
Living in your little bubble.
Living in your little world.
Are you happy?

Doing the same old things.
Saying the same old things.
Seeing the same old people.
Hearing the same old songs.
Eating the same old shit.
Going to the same old places.
Are you happy?

I don't see you around anymore.
Are you in hiding?
Are you in hibernation?
(It is winter & you've never liked the cold.)
(You're a beach babe, always have been, always will be).
You can take the girl out from the beach but you can't take the beach out of the girl).
So, are you happy?

"The Don"
28.05.2021

Wild Girls

(Ragazze Selvagge)

Wanna spend some time with 2 *"wild"* girls?
Wanna have a good time?
Bad girls.
Good girls gone bad.
They just wanna have fun.
There's nothing wrong with that.
You're just jealous...
.. because you're not a *"wild girl"*.

You know what you have to do.
You just gotta get rid of your inhibitions.
You've just gotta learn to be free.
You've just got *"live in the moment"*.
That's how you get to be a *"wild girl"*.

Take some risks.
Let your hair down.
Feel the music that's inside you.
Let the rhythm flow through your body.
Become loose.
That's how you become a *"wild girl"*.

"Wild girls" know how to have FUN.
"Wild girls" will drive you craaaaaaaaazzzzzy!
That's because they ARE craaaaaaaazzzzzy!
They have no limits.
They have no boundaries.

Are you ready?
Are you prepared?
Do you think you can handle her?
Because you'll be playing with fire.
When you play with *"wild girls"!*

All I can say is....
..."Good luck!"

Gooooooooooooooooooooo!
Grrrrrrrrrrrrrrrl POWER!

"The Don"
28.05.2021

"Wild Girls"
"Ceren" & "Yanet"
Photo taken, 27.05.2021

"Beach Girl"
Artist: Vanessa Wells
Insta: nesiw_
Email: nesiw@outlook.com

Bad Boy

(Cattivo Ragazzo)

I wanna be a bad boy.
I wanna be your sex toy.
I gonna give it a real good go.
I'm gonna give you a good show.
'cause I'm a bad boy.
I'm your sex toy.

I'm gonna let it all hang out.
I'm gonna make you shout.
I'm gonna give lots of pleasure.
You ain't gonna have any leisure.
I'm your sex toy.
'cause I'm a bad boy.

Wanna do a line?
I'm gonna give ya a good time.
I'll be your *"ManBag"*.
Babe, I'm gonna make ya so glad.
I'm your sex toy.
'cause I'm a bad boy.

I'm a real bad boy.
A bad, bad boy!
Bad boy, yes, I'm a bad boy.
I'm your sex toy.
'cause I'm a bad boy.

I'm a real bad boy.

We'll make LO♥E all night long.
I'll sing you all your favourite songs.
I gonna corrupt you.
But I'll never make you blue.
'cause I'm your sex toy.
I'm your bad boy.

I'm gonna make you implode.
You're gonna want to explode.
I'll push all the right buttons.
You don't have to do nothin'.
'cause I'm your sex toy.
I'm your bad boy.

I know the right spot.
I believe it's called the *"g"* spot.
I'm gonna make you wanna bend.
You'll never want it to end.
'cause I'm your sex toy.
'I'm your bad boy.

I'm a real bad boy.
A bad, bad boy!
Bad boy, yes, I'm a bad boy.
I'm your sex toy.
'cause I'm a bad boy.

I'm a real bad boy.
Bad boy.
I'm a bad, bad boy.

Bad boy.
I'm a bad, bad boy.

I'm a bad boy!
I'm a bad boy for Lo❤e!

I'm a real bad boy.
I'm a bad, bad boy.

Bad boy.
Talkin' about bad boy!
Yeah, Bad, bad boy!
Do you Lo❤e me?
'cause I'm a bad, bad boy!

(Inspired by the song "Bad Girls" sung by Donna Summer)

"The Don"
29.05.2021

Books written by "The Don"

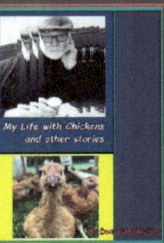

"My Life with Chickens & other stories: I Pity the Poor Immigrant"
Published:
10th September, 2019
Autobiography Book 1:
0 – 12 years old

"Poems for Misfits, Miscreants, Misanthropes, Mavericks, Losers & Malcontents!"
Published:
10th June, 2020
Book of Poems 1

"Poems for Troubled Minds & Trouble Hearts"
Published:
10th August, 2020
Book of Poems 2

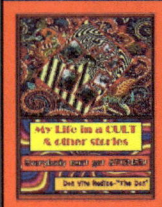

"My Life in a CULT & other stories: Everybody Must Get STONED!"
Published:
10th September, 2020
Autobiography Book 2:
15 – 30 years old

"Poems for Restless Minds & Restless Hearts"
Published:
10th October, 2020
Book of Poems 3

"Poems for Anarchists, Revolutionaries, Outlaws & Dissidents!"
Published:
10th November, 2020
Book of Poems 4

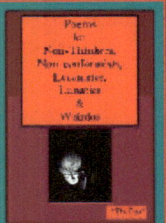

"Poems for Non-Thinkers & Eccentrics"
Published:
10th December, 2020
Book of Poems 5

"The Rantings of a Madman"
Published:
10th January, 2021
Book of Poems 6

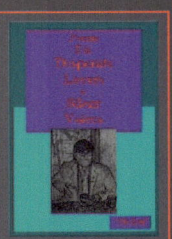

"Poems for Desperate Lovers & Silent Voices"
Published:
10th February, 2021
Book of Poems 7

"Poems for Tormented Minds & Tortured Souls"
Published:
10th March, 2021
Book of Poems 8

All available ONLY online

Books written by "The Don"

"Poems for ALIENS, Outsiders, Outcasts & other STRANGE BEINGS!"
Published: 10th April, 2021
Book of Poems 9

"Poems for Beings From Another Planet"
Published: 10th May, 2021
Book of Poems 10

"Poems for Mindless Beings & Lost Souls"
Published: 10th June, 2021
Book of Poems 11

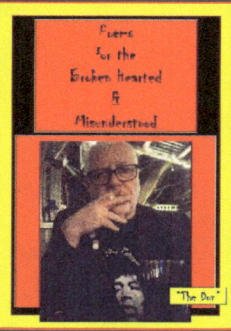

"Poems for the Broken Hearted & Misunderstood
Published: 10th July, 2021
Book of Poems 12

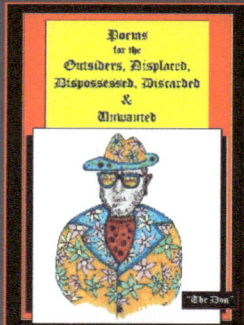

"Poems for Poems for the Bewildered, Dazed & Confused"
10th August, 2021

Book of Poems 13

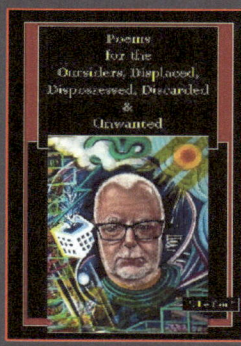

"Poems for the Outsiders, Displaced, Dispossessed, Discarded & Unwanted"
Published: 10th Sept, 2021
Book of Poems 14

All available ONLY online

Vito Radice ("The Don"):
Poet/Author/Polemicist/Non-Thinker/Non-Intellectual
To get in touch with Vito:
Email: vitoradice@gmail.com
Instagram: don_vito_radice
Facebook: Vito Radice
Mobile: +61490012461 (Australia)

www.ingramcontent.com/pod-product-compliance
Lightning Source LLC
Chambersburg PA
CBHW041502010526
44107CB00049B/1621

Acknowledgement of Land & of the Traditional Owners of this Land

I would like to acknowledge the Gadigal people of the Eora Nation, upon whose stolen land I stand on today.
I recognise that this land was never terra nullius — the land belonging to these peoples was never ceded, given up, bought or sold.
I would like to pay my respects to Aboriginal Elders past, present and emerging, and I extend this acknowledgement to all Aboriginal and Torres Strait Islander people.

This book is dedicated to those people that are bewildered, dazed & confused.
-"The Don"

Creative Disorder

It's about being NOT being controlled.
NOT being told what to do.
NOT being allowed to do what you want to do.
But being forced to do what someone else wants.
They get to decide for you.
They force you to do what they want.
Denying you your freedom to choose for yourself.
Forcing you to live according to their rules, their laws, which only serve them.
Thus, denying you your ability to express yourself freely.
Denying you the freedom to be creative.
Denying you the freedom to think.
Denying you the freedom to live the way YOU want to live.
Denying you your OWN life.

"The Don"
10.05.2021

"One of the most incredible energies I've felt in my life.
Uluru is culture.
Uluru is amazing.
Uluru is ancestry.
Uluru is magic.
Uluru is feeling."

-Anna, 18.06.2021

"Uluru"
Sacred site of Australian First Nations People
A place of enormous spiritual & cultural Significance
Photos taken, by Anna, June 2021